CLASSICAL FAVORITES

10 of the World's Most Treasured Masterpieces
Arranged for Intermediate to Late Intermediate Pianists

Sharon Aaronson

There are a number of outstanding classical masterpieces that we love to hear again and again. Much of this music is not written for piano, and a lot of the repertoire composed expressly for piano is technically challenging. Now, with the intermediate- through late-intermediate-level arrangements in *Top 10 Classical Favorites,* some of the world's favorite piano, orchestral and operatic masterpieces are right at your fingertips.

This collection includes music by nine celebrated composers from all musical style periods— Pachelbel, J. S. Bach, Mozart, Beethoven, Chopin, Puccini, Debussy, Joplin and Rachmaninoff. These arrangements can be played simply for your own enjoyment, at informal gatherings, and are perfect for recitals. I hope you find as much pleasure in performing these pieces as I did in arranging them for you.

Sharon Aaronson

to my husband, Alan, with love

Jesu, Joy of Man's Desiring

from *Cantata No. 147*

Johann Sebastian Bach (1685–1750)
Arr. by Sharon Aaronson

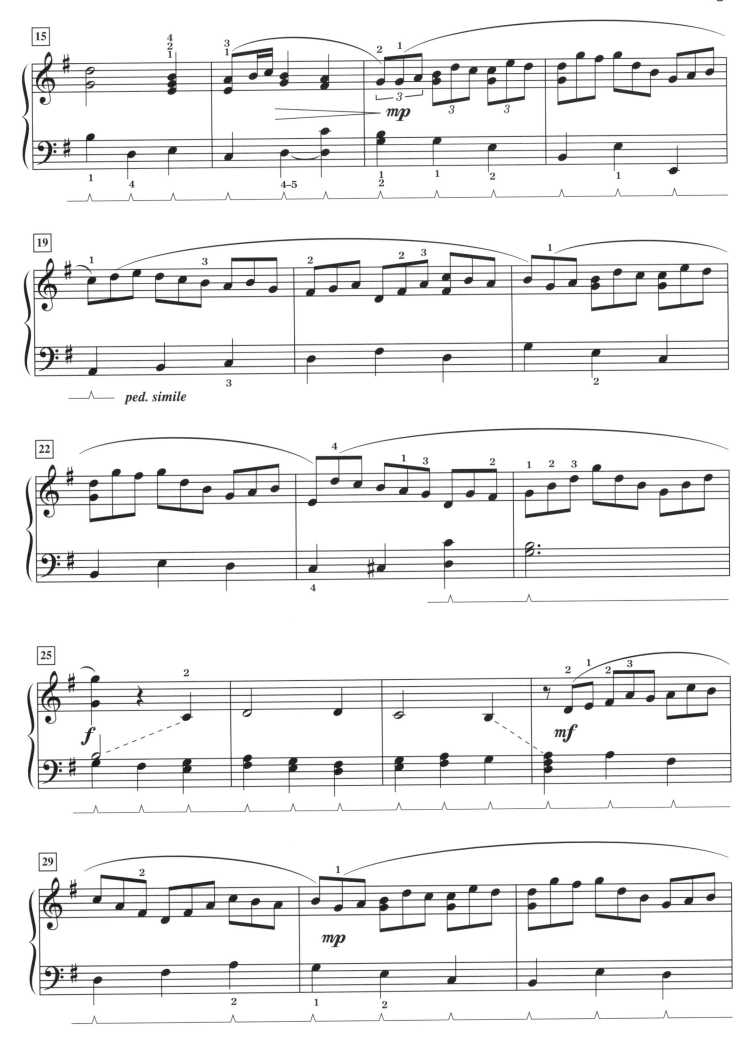

ped. simile

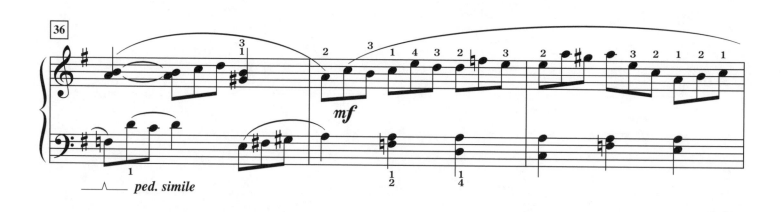

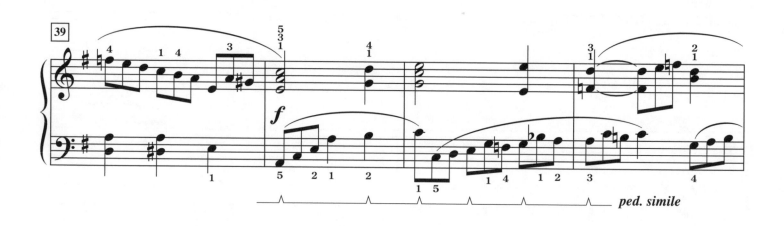

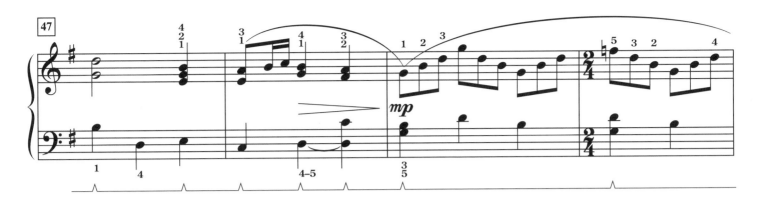

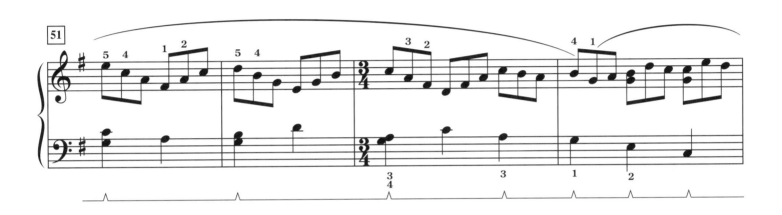

Canon in D

Johann Pachelbel (1653–1706)
Arr. by Sharon Aaronson

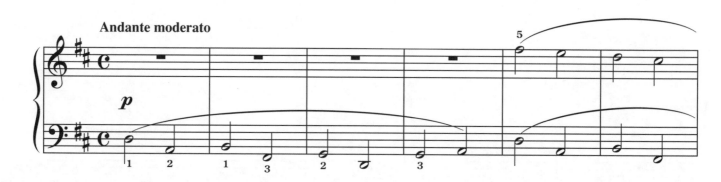

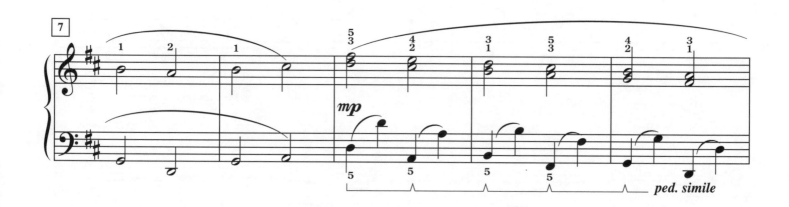

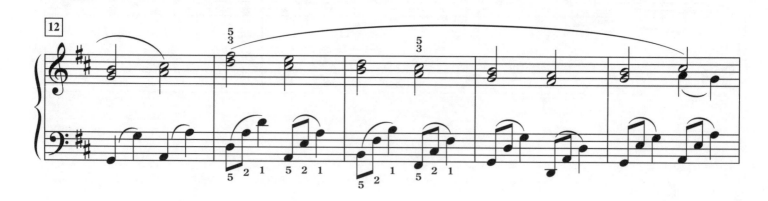

Moonlight Sonata

First Movement

Ludwig van Beethoven (1770–1827)
Op. 27, No. 2
Arr. by Sharon Aaronson

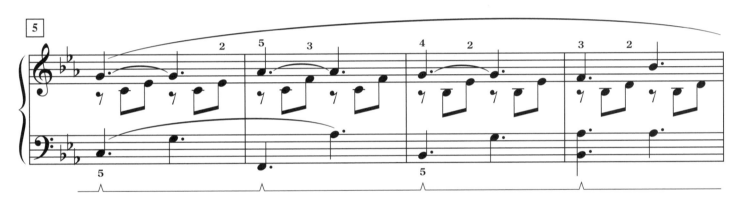

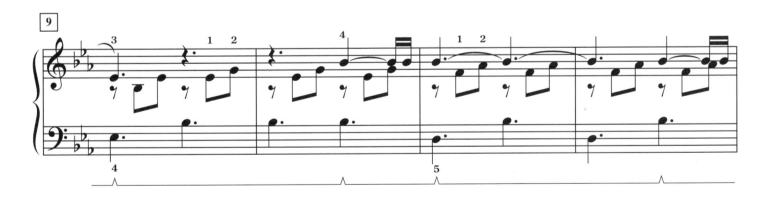

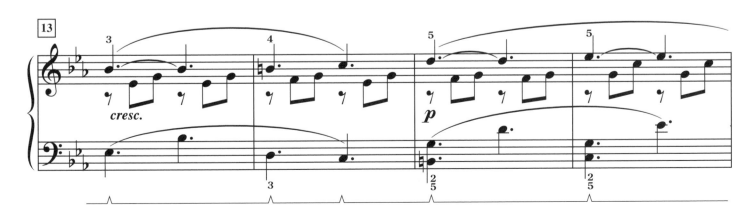

Ode to Joy

from *Symphony No. 9*

Ludwig van Beethoven (1770–1827)
Op. 125
Arr. by Sharon Aaronson

Allegro

from *Eine kleine Nachtmusik*

Wolfgang Amadeus Mozart (1756–1791)
K. 525
Arr. by Sharon Aaronson

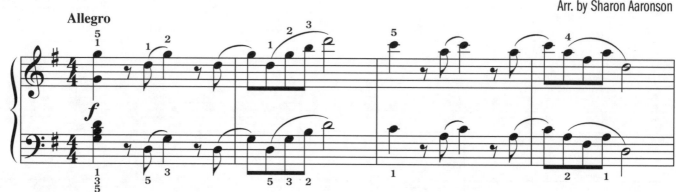

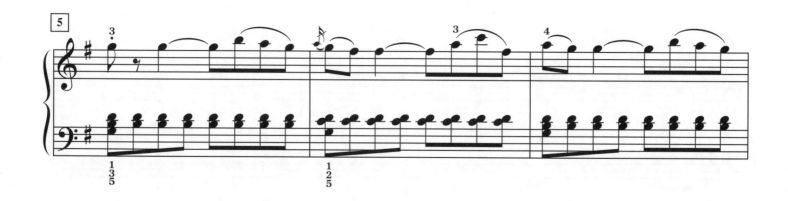

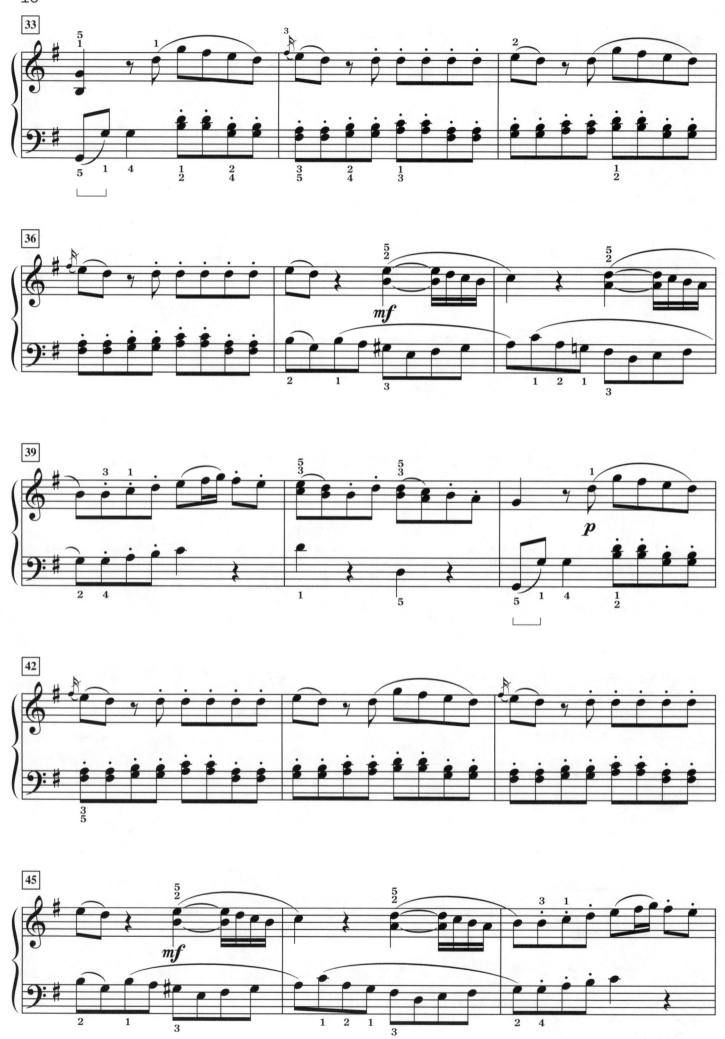

Marche funèbre

from *Sonata No. 2*

Frédéric François Chopin (1810–1849)
Op. 35
Arr. by Sharon Aaronson

Nessun dorma

from *Turandot*

Giacomo Puccini (1858–1924)
Arr. by Sharon Aaronson

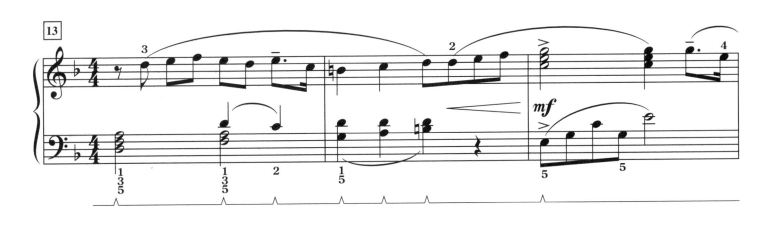

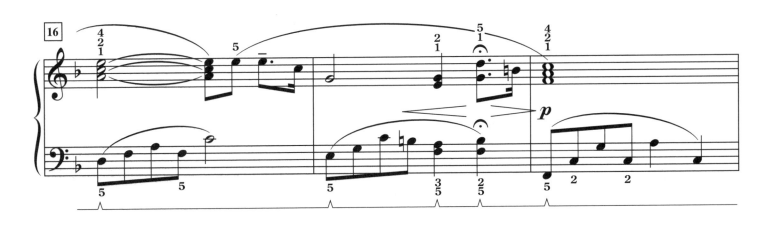

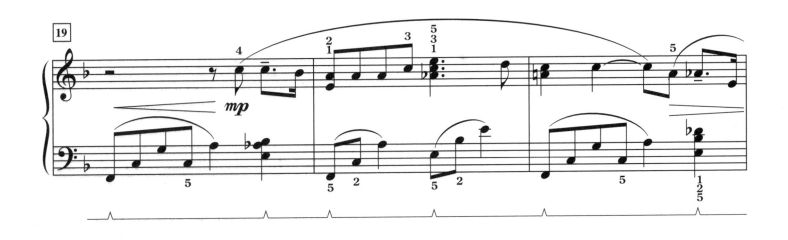

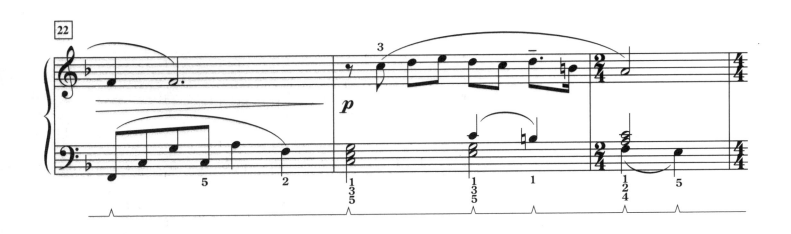

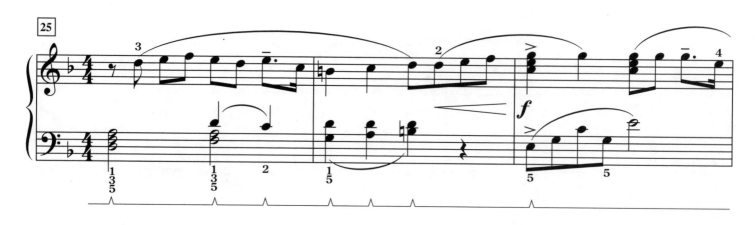

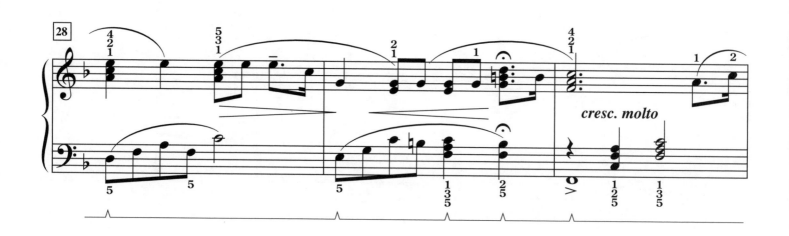

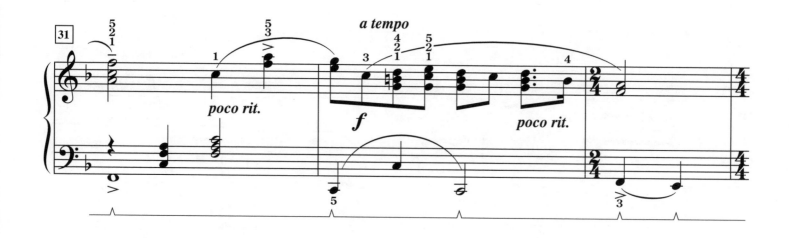

Clair de lune

from *Suite Bergamasque*

Claude Debussy (1862–1918)
Arr. by Sharon Aaronson

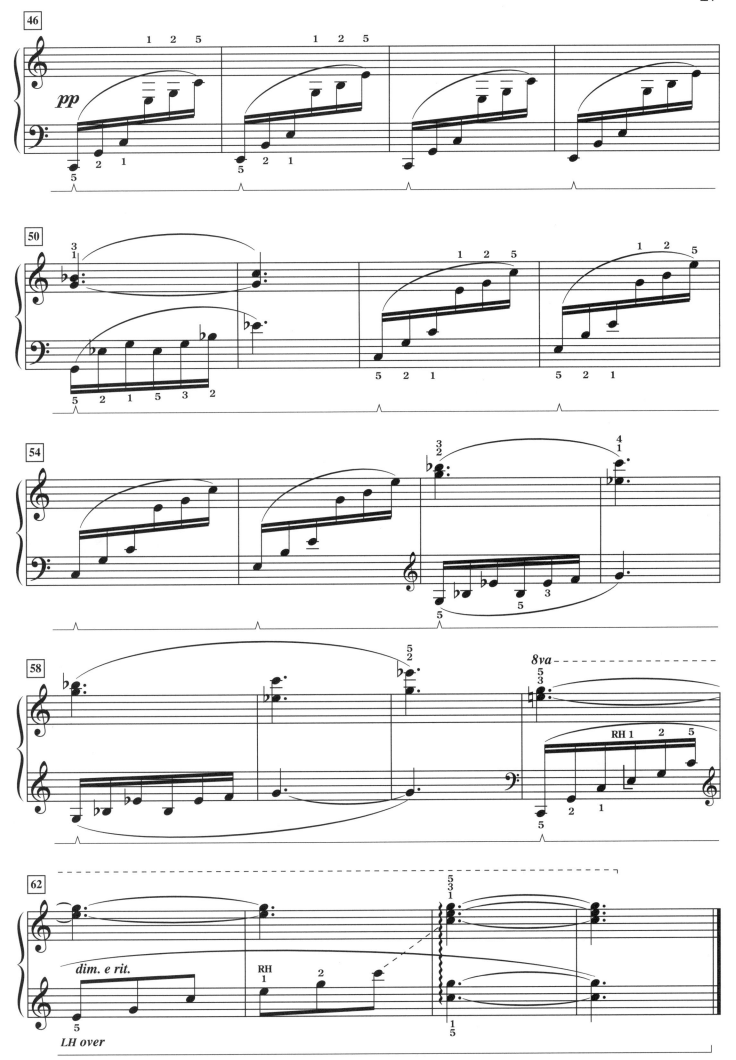

The Entertainer

A Ragtime Two-Step

Scott Joplin (1868–1917)
Arr. by Sharon Aaronson

Rhapsody

on a Theme of Paganini

Sergei Rachmaninoff (1873–1943)
Op. 43
Arr. by Sharon Aaronson

Andante cantabile

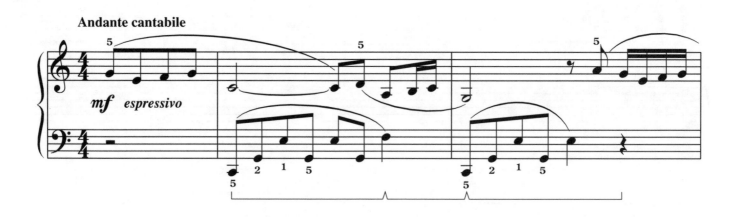

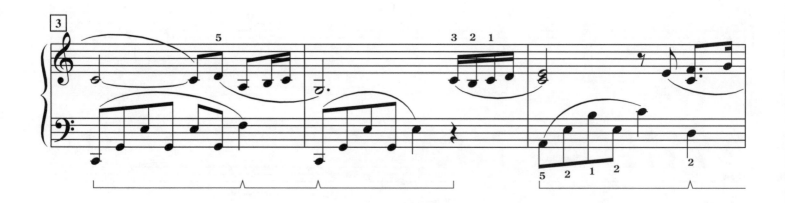

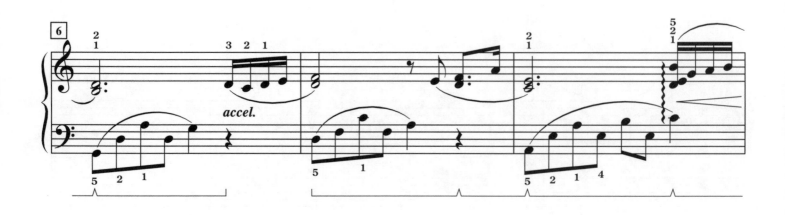

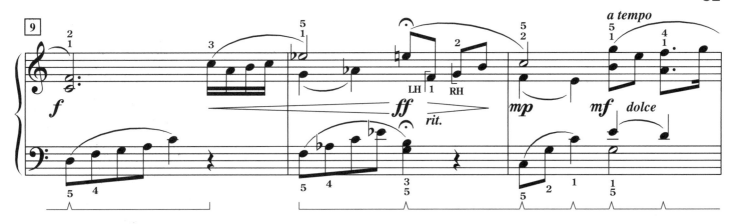

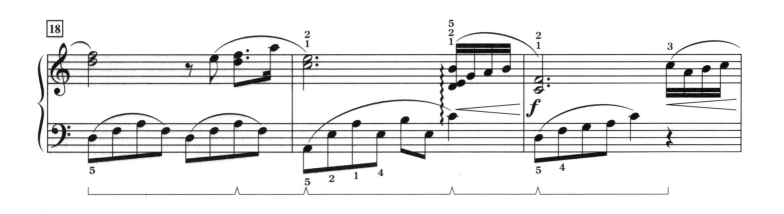

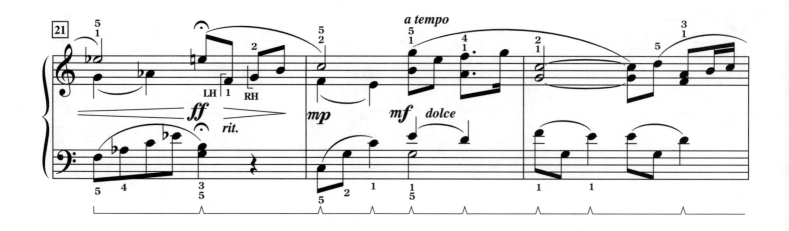

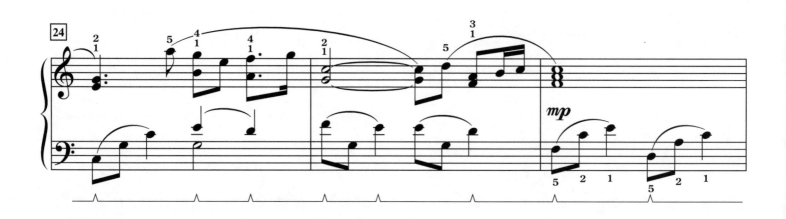

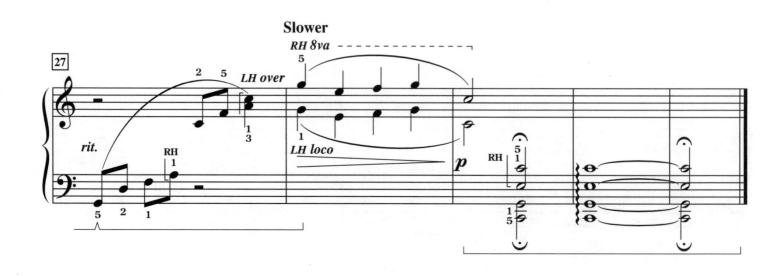